Ladybird  Readers

Mountains

Series Editor: Sorrel Pitts
Written by Rachel Godfrey

LADYBIRD BOOKS

UK | USA | Canada | Ireland | Australia
India | New Zealand | South Africa

Ladybird Books is part of the Penguin Random House group of companies
whose addresses can be found at global.penguinrandomhouse.com.
www.penguin.co.uk   www.puffin.co.uk   www.ladybird.co.uk

Penguin
Random House
UK

First published 2018
001
Text copyright © Ladybird Books Ltd, 2018

All images copyright © BBC, 2006
Cover photograph by Tom Hugh-Jones copyright © BBC NHU, 2016
BBC and BBC Earth (word marks and logos) are trade marks of the
British Broadcasting Corporation and are used under licence.
BBC logo © BBC 1996. BBC Earth logo © 2014.

Printed in China

A CIP catalogue record for this book is available from the British Library

ISBN: 978-0-241-31948-2

All correspondence to:
Ladybird Books
Penguin Random House Children's
80 Strand, London WC2R 0RL

MIX
Paper from
responsible sources
FSC® C018179
www.fsc.org

Ladybird Readers

Mountains

Inspired by BBC Earth TV series and
developed with input from BBC Earth
natural history specialists

Contents

Picture words   6

Mountain ranges
of the world   8

Living in the mountains   10

Gelada baboons   12

Snow leopards   16

Demoiselle cranes   20

Problems for
our mountains   24

Our mountains
are important   26

Activities   28

Picture words

mountain

mountain range

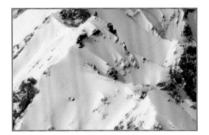

snow

ice

gelada baboon

guanaco

wolves

snow leopard

demoiselle
crane

bears

markhor

Mountain ranges of the world

the Rockies

the Andes

There are many mountain ranges on Earth.

Read about these mountain ranges in this book.

the Himalayas

the Ethiopian
Highlands

Living in the mountains

It is difficult for animals to live in the mountains. The weather is often very hot or very cold, and there is not much food.

Gelada baboons live in the Ethiopian Highlands.

gelada baboon

bear

Bears live in the Rockies.

snow leopard

Snow leopards live in the Himalayas.

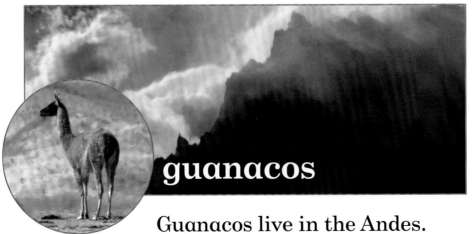

guanacos

Guanacos live in the Andes.

11

Gelada baboons

Gelada baboons
live together in the
Ethiopian Highlands.

The gelada baboons' strong fingers help them to climb on the mountains.

Many baboons like eating fruit, but there is no fruit in these mountains.

Lots of grass grows in the Ethiopian Highlands. Gelada baboons eat lots of grass here.

grass

Wolves live in the Ethiopian Highlands, too.

These baboons know the wolves are near.

Snow leopards

There are snow leopards
in the Himalayas.
Snow leopards catch
and eat other animals.

Animals cannot hear or see snow leopards in the snow. The leopards can run very fast to catch other animals.

This snow leopard is hungry.

A markhor is a big goat with big horns.

The snow leopard sees a young markhor. The snow leopard runs after it.

The markhor
runs down the
mountain.

The leopard
cannot catch
the markhor.

The markhor is
safe in the river.

19

Demoiselle cranes

Every year, 50,000 demoiselle cranes fly across the Himalayas.

These cranes must fly to India for the winter.

The weather changes
quickly in the mountains.
It is difficult to fly in
bad weather.

Today, the weather is good.
The cranes can fly today.

Problems for our mountains

Mountains have a lot of problems. Snow and ice are changing to water. People are taking the trees.

This is bad for the animals in the mountains. Many animals have their homes in the mountains.

Birds live in the trees in the mountains.

The red panda finds food in the mountains.

Our mountains are important

Many birds and animals need our mountains.

We must help them.
We can help them by taking
fewer trees and taking litter
home from the mountains.

Activities

The key below describes the skills practiced in each activity.

 Spelling and writing

 Reading

 Speaking

Critical thinking

Preparation for the Cambridge Young Learners exams

1 **Match the words to the pictures.**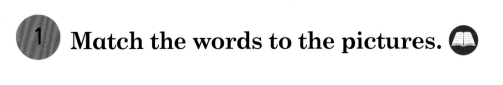

1 baboon

2 crane

3 bear

4 wolf

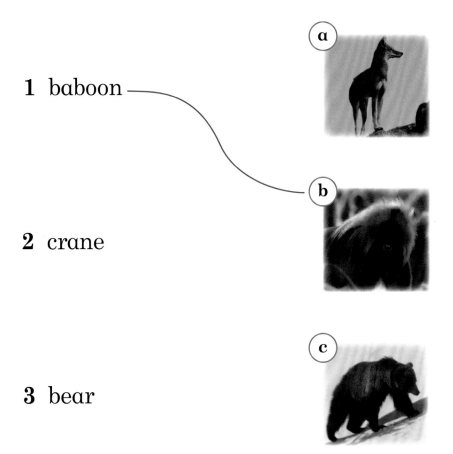

2 Look and read. Write *yes* or *no*.

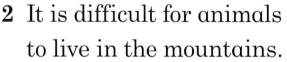
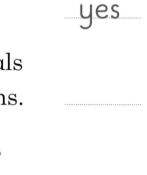

Living in the mountains

It is difficult for animals to live in the mountains. The weather is often very hot or very cold, and there is not much food.

Gelada baboons live in the Ethiopian Highlands.

gelada baboon

bear

Bears live in the Rockies.

snow leopard

Snow leopards live in the Himalayas.

guanacos

Guanacos live in the Andes.

10   11

1 Animals live in the mountains.   yes

2 It is difficult for animals to live in the mountains. ....

3 The weather is always cold in the mountains. ....

4 There is a lot of food in the mountains. ....

3 Talk to a friend about animals in the mountains. 🗨

1

> *Where do gelada baboons live?*

> *They live in the Ethiopian Highlands.*

2 Which animals live in the Rockies?

3 Which animals live in the Himalayas?

4 Which animals live in the Andes?

4 Match and write the names of the mountain ranges.

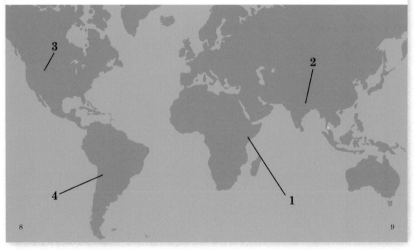

Mountain ranges of the world

There are many mountain ranges on Earth.

Read about these mountain ranges in this book.

1 the Ethiopian Highlands

2

3

4

5 Circle the correct words.

1 These are **snow leopards. /** ~~gelada baboons.~~

2 Gelada baboons live **together. / in the snow.**

3 They live in the **Rockies. / Ethiopian Highlands.**

4 Gelada baboons have strong **legs. / fingers.**

6 **Find the words.**

a	s	t	r	o	n	g	f
b	p	o	l	p	f	d	u
a	g	g	j	l	i	v	e
b	f	e	g	t	n	j	o
o	c	t	t	w	g	s	w
o	n	h	r	d	e	k	l
n	b	e	b	n	r	h	m
t	a	r	h	u	s	a	f

live   strong   baboon
fingers   together

7 Look and read. Put a  or a X in the boxes.

1  This is grass.

2  This is a baboon. ☐

3  These are baboons. ☐

4  This is a mountain. ☐

8 **Look at the pictures.**
Write the answers. 📖 ✏️ ⬡

Many baboons like eating fruit, but there is no fruit in these mountains.

Lots of grass grows in the Ethiopian Highlands. Gelada baboons eat lots of grass here.

grass

Wolves live in the Ethiopian Highlands, too.

These baboons know the wolves are near.

15

1 These animals are baboons and .... wolves ....

2 They live in the

....

3 There is no ....
to eat in these mountains.

4 Gelada baboons eat lots of
.... here.

5 The baboons know the
.... are near.

9 **Ask and answer the questions with a friend.** 💬 ❓

1

> *What are these animals?*

> *They are snow leopards.*

2 Where do they live?

3 What are they doing?

4 Do you like snow leopards?
Why? / Why not?

10 **Write the correct sentences.**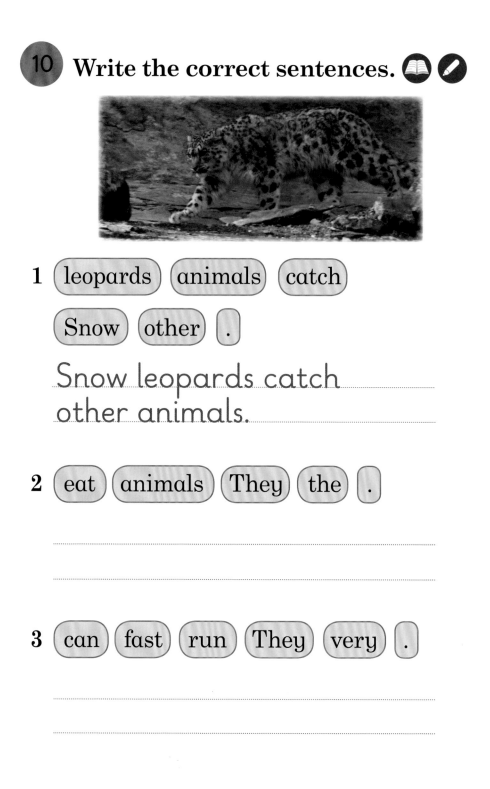

1 (leopards) (animals) (catch)
  (Snow) (other) (.)

Snow leopards catch
other animals.

2 (eat) (animals) (They) (the) (.)

3 (can) (fast) (run) (They) (very) (.)

11 Circle the correct words.

1 The snow leopard sees a
   a young markhor.
   b young baboon.

2 The snow leopard . . . the markhor.
   a looks at
   b runs after

3 The markhor runs
   a down the mountain.
   b to the snow leopard.

4 The snow leopard
   a can catch the markhor.
   b cannot catch the markhor.

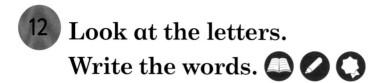

12 **Look at the letters.**
Write the words.

1 (k r h o a m r)

A _markhor_ is a big, brown animal.

2 (r s e l p a o d)

Animals cannot hear snow _____
in the snow.

3 (n o u t n a i m)

The markhor runs down the
_____ from the leopard.

13 Complete the sentences.
Write a—c.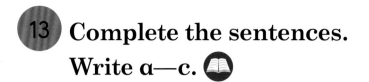

1 These animals are ....c........

2 Every year, demoiselle
cranes ....

3 They fly ....

---

a fly across the Himalayas.

b to India.

c demoiselle cranes.

14 **Read the questions.
Write short answers.** 📖 ✏️ ❓

The weather changes quickly in the mountains. It is difficult to fly in bad weather.

Today, the weather is good. The cranes can fly today.

1 Does the weather change in the mountains?

Yes, it does.

2 Is it easy to fly in bad weather?

3 Can the cranes travel fast in good weather? Why? / Why not?

15 **Find the words.**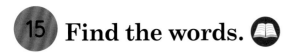

t k d w e a t h e r n g a p d c h a n g e b j p o f n d i f f i c u l t s b f l y a t h d n o p l t r a v e l h l m p o s v d c r a n e

weather

travel

change

difficult

fly

crane

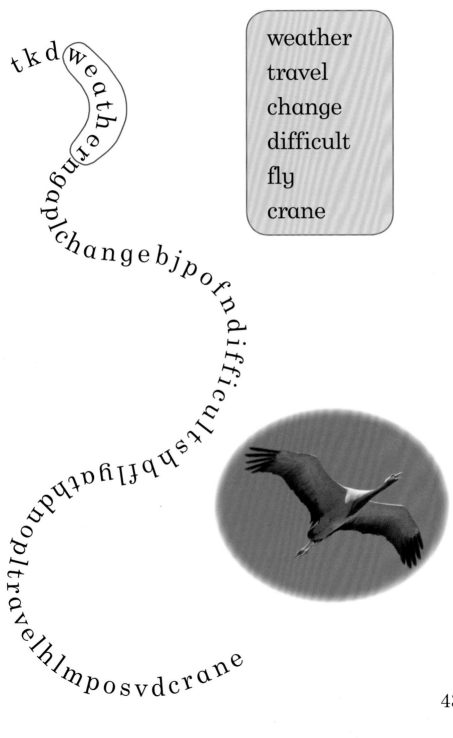

16 **Circle the correct pictures.**

1 This animal can run very fast.

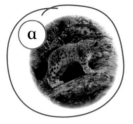
a

b

2 Baboons eat this.

a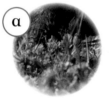

b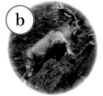

3 This animal flies to India for winter.

a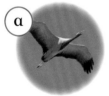

b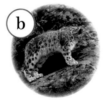

4 This animal has strong fingers.

a

b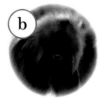

17 **Write *T* (true) or *F* (false).**

Problems for our mountains

Mountains have a lot of problems. Snow and ice are changing to water. People are taking the trees.

This is bad for the animals in the mountains. Many animals have their homes in the mountains.

Birds live in the trees in the mountains.

The red panda finds food in the mountains.

24

25

1 Mountains have a lot of problems. ....T............

2 There is too much snow and ice in the mountains. ....

3 People are taking trees from the mountains. ....

4 This is good for the animals in the mountains. ....

18 **Circle the correct words.** 📖

1 Many animals have their
   (homes)/ **friends** in the mountains.

2 Birds live in the **snow** / **trees**
   in the mountains.

3 The red panda finds **food** / **flowers**
   in the mountains.

4 **Fish** / **Bears** live in the mountains.

19 Put a ☑ by all the animals in this book. 📖

1	baboons	✔	**2**	bears	☐
3	sheep	☐	**4**	wolves	☐
5	dogs	☐	**6**	leopards	☐
7	lions	☐	**8**	cranes	☐
9	eagles	☐	**10**	guanacos	☐
11	markhor	☐	**12**	fish	☐
13	red pandas	☐	**14**	kangaroos	☐

Level 2

The Gingerbread Man	Sly Fox and Red Hen	The Monster Next Door	Wild Animals	Little Red Riding Hood
978-0-241-25442-4 ☐	978-0-241-25443-1 ☐	978-0-241-25444-8 ☐	978-0-241-25445-5 ☐	978-0-241-25446-2 ☐
Dinosaurs	Topsy and Tim The Big Race	Goes to the Treehouse	Sports Day	Going on a Picnic
978-0-241-25447-9 ☐	978-0-241-25448-6 ☐	978-0-241-25449-3 ☐	978-0-241-26222-1 ☐	978-0-241-26221-4 ☐
Peter Rabbit and the Angry Owl	Superhero Max	We Can Help!	Daddy Pig's New Van	School Trip
978-0-241-28369-1 ☐	978-0-241-28368-4 ☐	978-0-241-28367-7 ☐	978-0-241-28371-4 ☐	978-0-241-28372-1 ☐
The Peter Rabbit Club	Daddy Pig's Office	Spring is Here!	Great Trains	Hungry Animals
978-0-241-29811-4 ☐	978-0-241-29814-5 ☐	978-0-241-29809-1 ☐	978-0-241-29808-4 ☐	978-0-241-29844-2 ☐
Mountains	In a Plane	Playing Football	Grimlock Stops the Decepticons	
978-0-241-31948-2 ☐	978-0-241-31945-1 ☐	978-0-241-31947-5 ☐	978-0-241-31954-3 ☐	

Now you're ready for Level 3!